ISBN: 9781691817443

Imprint: Independently published
Published by Civin Media Relations
www.civinmediarelations.com

Printed in the United States

El Correcaminos

Written by Todd Civin ~ Illustrated by Eva Anziano

Dedication

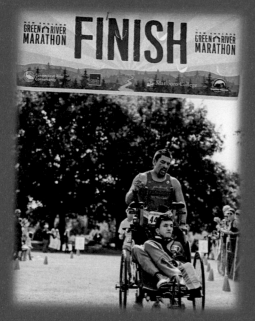

I would like to dedicate this book to my beautiful wife Virgen, my wonderful children Angel and Sam and to my many friends, family and followers who are making this journey possible. I'd also like to dedicate the book to Team Hoyt New England and especially to our founders <u>Dick Hoyt</u> and <u>Rick Hoyt</u>, who are teaching the world the meaning of Yes You Can!

<u>www.civinmediarelations.com</u>

Me gustaría dedicar este libro a mi bella esposa Virgen, mis maravillosos hijos Angel y Sam y a mis muchos amigos, familiares y seguidores que están haciendo posible este viaje. También me gustaría dedicar el libro al Equipo Hoyt New England y especialmente a nuestros fundadores Dick Hoyt y Rick Hoyt, que están enseñando al mundo el significado de ¡Sí, puedes!

<u>www.civinmediarelations.com</u>

~ Hiram Cruz

The road of life takes curves at times,
Not always as expected.
But with love and faith and hope and prayer,
His plan becomes perfected.

Blessed slightly after New Year's Day,
In the year two thousand three.
Came the entrance a special child.
Though affected by CP.

The boy was born with challenges,
But was filled with so much love.
His parents named him Angel,
Like a gift from up above.

The family included him,
Treated just like any other.
Jenitza and Hiram would bring him up,
With Sam his younger brother.

Sam is like a young adult,
With kindness, grace and charm.
A knight in shining army,
Keeps Angel safe from harm.

El Correcaminos

As the two boys grew much older,
Dad took Sammy for a run.
Why don't you include Angel?
To join into your fun.

They found a race called Colorfest
Where the family became acquainted,
Angel clapped and laughed as each of them,
Became so brightly painted.

Though the papa's name is Hiram,

Angel and Sam are the ninos.

With great help from their Madre,

They're now known as El Correcaminos.

They're quicker than a roadrunner,
Fastest trio upon three wheels.
The harder Dad and Sammy push,
The louder Angel squeals.

They learned of another
duo team,
Who taught the world inclusion,
When Angel's running he's
not disabled,
They have come to the
conclusion.

Dick and Rick Hoyt carved the path,
For others to run behind.
Angel and Sammy spread their message,
That they teach to human kind.

Does not matter what life hands you,
You must face it with a smile.
Just share a Yes You Can view of life
While enjoying every mile.

And one more lesson before we end,

Which we learned from El Correcaminos,

Is treat everyone with kindness,

Y ama a tu projimo.

About the Author

Todd Civin is a husband, father of five and grandfather of four to date. He is a graduate of Syracuse University Newhouse School of Public Communications. Todd is the owner and creator of Civin Media Relations and is the Social Media Director for the Kyle Pease Foundation and The Hoyt Foundation.

He is the co-author of One Letter at a Time by Rick Hoyt and Todd Civin, Destined to Run by Wes Harding and Todd Civin, Just My Game by MLB pitcher Jason Grilli and Todd Civin Line Change by Matt Brown and Todd Civin and Beyond the Finish by Brent and Kyle Pease and Todd Civin. He is also the author and creator of fourteen children's books including, Where There's a Wheel There's a Way and A Knight in Shining Armor, A Bike to Call Their Own and Together We Finish! He is thrilled to add El Correcaminos to his book shelf.

The creation of Civin Media Relations is his absolute pleasure allowing all those associated with the team to provide positive exposure to those who are different or differently-abled. To be able to share the talents of like-minded individuals provides him with an indescribable sense of fulfillment and personal satisfaction.

About the Artist

Eva Anziano is a self-taught artist, who resides between Poland and the United States. She specializes in realistic sketches and pyrography.

She is the mother of two children, Dennis, age 10, and Zoë, age 2. This is her first opportunity to participate in a children's book project and she's excited to add El Correcaminos to her portfolio of work.

Her art can be found at https://m.facebook.com/evaanzianofineart/

Todd Civin

Owner and Publisher

www.civinmediarelations.com

2 Robbins Rd, Winchendon, MA 01475

978-502-1453